BO

THE JOURNEY OF LIFE. YOU ARE ON THIS AMAZING, POWERFUL JOURNEY. YOU ARE IN THE PROCESS OF CHIPPING AWAY WHAT NO LONGER SERVES YOU TO REVEAL YOUR SENSUAL, CREATIVE, POWERFUL, AUTHENTIC SELF.

THIS SMALL HANDBOOK WILL RE-ESTABLISH YOUR CONNECTION TO THE WISE WOMAN INSIDE OF ALL WOMEN. I HOPE THESE INSPIRATIONS AND ACTIVITIES AWAKEN THE CIRCLE OF WISDOM WITHIN YOU. EMBRACE THIS JOURNEY. TRUST THE PROCESS. ALLOW YOURSELF TO BECOME MORE THAN YOU EVER DREAMED YOU COULD BE. LIVE WITH PASSION, PURPOSE, AND CLARITY EACH DAY. THE WORLD AWAITS YOU!

SUZY MANNING

We know that life is a journey to celebrate and enjoy.
Detours offer unexpected opportunities for growth.

Just for today, follow a detour to see where it leads. Celebrate what you learn about yourself and your life by traveling down an unexpected road.

Nurturing ourselves is our #1 priority.
We understand that we have to be full in order
to give to others.

Define one thing that you would like to do for yourself today. Something simple: read a chapter in a novel, pick a flower, take a walk, stretch. Make the time to pursue this need and enjoy celebrating who you are.

Giving voice to our thoughts is not an option, it is who we are. We stand firm and speak with a voice of power, we are proud to be seen and heard.

Speak one truth that you need to express from your heart without concern whether anyone else agrees or supports your viewpoint.

Women following their passion have an inner glow and infectious energy. We follow our inner voice and dance our dreams awake.

Take the time to sit in a quiet space and listen to your inner voice. Take a first step to becoming the woman you want to be. Celebrate the warm fuzzy feeling within as you embrace your true self.

As wise women, we evolve from birthing children to caretakers of the Universe. Our voices calm, our touch soothes, our arms comfort, as our bodies radiate energy contagious to all.

Spend some time in nature noticing how it re-energizes you and helps you to prioritize what really matters in your life. Embrace a project that feeds both you and humanity.

We each cultivate our own inner garden knowing we are meant to bloom to create a larger harmonious, sensual bouquet known as humanity.

What is your favorite flower? How are you like this flower? What color flower are you? What is your scent? How do you fit into the bouquet of life?

In leadership, we view everyone as an integral part of the solution. We value connecting to, caring for, and taking responsibility for mediating change.

Today, help someone see that there are many different ways of viewing, embracing, and growing from change.

Feminine power is soft power. We view power in terms of being strong in order to help, share, and empower others.

Become aware of how you interact with others. Today, give something (a hug, compliment, a listening ear, support) without expecting anything in return.

No is a complete sentence. We don't have to take care of everything and everyone all of the time.

Say no to something today without an explanation and notice that the world does not end. Life goes on.

We can wear anything and people say "Oh, you look great!" It is not the clothing, the makeup, or the accessories, but our energy that creates the look.

Look at yourself in the mirror seeing your beauty without makeup.
Look at your body and see its beauty and energy. Every one is beautiful just as they are.

We love who we are, the journey we are on,
and life itself, and it shows.

Compliment a friend or a stranger today without expecting anything in return.

We have our own individual style created by each of us that serves our lifestyle. It speaks to comfort, creativity, and chic.

Wear an outfit today that you have always wanted to wear. Wear it with confidence that says, "I know who I am and I love who I am."

Solutions for us are SOULutions. Every action supports our inner growth toward realizing our divine purpose.

Schedule time everyday to pursue what it is that makes you lose all track of time. You will have more energy at the end of your day, by taking little steps everyday to live your purpose.

Who we think we are is who we become.
We never allow anyone to negate who we are
or to sabotage our dreams.

Today, be the person that you want to become. See what it feels like. Know that you can be this person at any time. Believe in you!

Our thought process creates our reality. What we believe we can accomplish, we accomplish.

Embrace one thing today that you would like to accomplish and do whatever it takes to make it happen. Celebrate your success and notice how much easier it is to do than you had imagined.

Fear is never the monster we make it out to be.
We conquer our fears by stepping into them,
experiencing them, and walking through them.

Face one of your fears today, move through it, and then celebrate your accomplishment.

Thin does not equate to health or beauty. Living with passion and purpose creates a healthy body and a presence that draws people to us.

Do you have a purpose in your life that gets your juices flowing every day? If you could not fail, what would you be doing with your life? Start today!

Our bodies are always trying to maintain balance. We listen to our body and seek resolution before stress or discomfort turns into illness and disease.

Take time today to slow down long enough to assess if you are really living your life or someone else's plan for your life. Your health depends on it!

We keep our heart healthy by engaging in life from our heartspace. We live, feel, and speak what resonates in our heart.

Connect with a vision that brings joy to your heart. Feel it, talk about it, and live it 24/7. Bring more joy into your life.

Buying things for self and others to gain approval, acceptance, and happiness has one result: debt. Debt in our bank account and debt in our body's energy reserve.

Just for today, give to yourself and others – time, kindness, love, and a listening ear.
Notice how energized your life becomes.

We understand that all of our stories overlap. We all want to be loved and accepted for who we are, not for a title or a bank account.

Talk with someone today that you would not normally connect with. Hear your story in her story.

We see beauty in older women. The soft wrinkles and satin skin represent understanding, truth, dignity, and yes, wisdom.

Connect with an older woman who celebrates her age and feel the power in aging with beauty and wisdom.

We embrace our past, because without having lived it we would not be the women we are today.

Journal a timeline of events in your life noting how each event has led you to where you are now. See the patterns you were unaware of at the time.

Laughter keeps us young, vibrant, and healthy and the sparkle in our eyes always keeps others wondering… what we are up to.

Today, get in touch with your inner child.
Skip down the street, tell a silly story, laugh for the pure joy of feeling alive!

New adventures, new ideas, and new experiences energize us. We welcome life with open arms and an open mind.

Step into a new situation today open to whatever challenges it brings. Embrace it as a chance to discover more about yourself and your life.

We understand that we cannot change anyone.
We can only choose to change ourselves.

Today, instead of attempting to change a person or a situation, change your perception or approach to a person or an event. Would you rather be right, or happy?

Life is a process. We are in process. Who we are today is different than who we were yesterday and who we will be tomorrow.

How are you doing things differently than you did one year ago? How have your priorities changed? How are you different than one month ago?
One week ago?
Yesterday?

We are right where we need to be to learn what it is we need to learn in life. What we need to work on will follow us wherever we go.

Doing the same old thing over and over again expecting different results keeps us stuck. What do you need to change in your life to move forward?

We realize that who we are defines our career, not vice versa. We define our lives. We do not allow life to define who we are.

Do you jump out of bed every morning excited about a new venture or project in your life? If not, clarify what it is you want to do with your life and create that reality.

Everything that has happened in our life was part of our journey to sculpt us into powerful, wise women.

Take the time to reflect on events that happened in your life and see how they shaped who you are today.

We eat to live, not live to eat! We honor our bodies by eating only enough to nurture us.

If you are living to eat, get in touch with what is eating you. What are you trying to soothe with food – anger, resentment, sadness, boredom, loss of meaning in your life? Fill yourself up with your dreams and take action.

Pursuing our purpose in life energizes us.
We have more energy at the end of the day
than at the beginning.

Track your energy level for a week and notice the difference in your energy at the end of the day when you are involved in activities that support you.

We know that what we put our attention on
e x p a n d s .

This morning put an intent into the Universe and then watch who and what appears in your life today.

To gain more money, more happiness, or more opportunity in our lives, we know that we have to be grateful for what exists in our lives currently.

Every night before you go to bed, make a gratitude list. Notice that when you are truly grateful for what you have in your life, more will appear in your life.

We embrace change as an integral part of our journey. We know that nothing is static. It is either growing or it is decaying.

Where in your life do you need to grow? Grass doesn't try to grow; it just grows. Flowers don't try to bloom; they just bloom. Allow yourself a small growth spurt today. Notice how alive you feel.

We welcome chaos into our lives as a powerful time for growth: physical, mental, emotional, and spiritual.

Embrace what is chaotic in your life right now. Where have you become complacent in your life? What needs to change? Thank your chaotic experience for humbling you and bringing balance into your life!

We engage with all of life. We experience life in the moment. We smell it, sense it, taste it, observe it, feel it, and hear it.

Today, experience everything on your path.
Do not just travel from point A to point B unaware.
Life is what happens between these points.

We know that we are responsible for our own health, our wealth, and our happiness.

Take steps today to be in supportive relationships.
self
career
family
Eat healthy, exercise, create your own income stream. Invest in yourself.

The woman warrior resides in each of us.
She engages us with her wit, her wisdom,
her sincere caring, and her sensuality.

*Celebrate the qualities that make you unique.
Notice when you embrace your naturalness you
naturally draw people to you. You command your space.
This is the warrior.*

We have many hungers that we must feed to be energetic and well. Our mental, physical, emotional, spiritual, and sexual cravings must all be nourished.

Read a book. Go back to school. Sign up for a dance class.
Move your body. Speak from your heart. Meditate.
Do yoga. Enjoy touch. Delight in orgasms.
Explore creative expression. Celebrate all of you!
You are amazing!

Grandmother Earth draped in the white beauty of winter is vibrant beneath the gaze of our roving eyes. So too is the reserved, white haired grandmother alive with gifts to offer the world.

Spend some time with an older woman and listen with your entire body to the wisdom she has to share. Incorporate a piece of her knowledge into your life and notice the difference it makes.

Suzy Manning is a professional trainer and a published author. Her passionate teachings for women on living their life with purpose come from her heart and from her own journey to discover and live her own dreams. She has a Masters Degree in Counseling and is an avid seeker of wisdom and tools to empower women.

Suzy lives in Arizona with her husband, Fuzzy. She loves creating new relationships, & being part of an organic, heart-centered community impacting lives internationally. Contact Suzy at 313.820.9265 or at susankaymanning@gmail.com